EZEKIEL ELLIOTT

SUPERSTAR RUNNING BACK

BIG BUDDY

★ NFL ★
SUPERSTARS

Big Buddy Books
An Imprint of Abdo Publishing
abdobooks.com

DENNIS ST. SAUVER

abdobooks.com

Published by Abdo Publishing, a division of ABDO, PO Box 398166, Minneapolis, Minnesota 55439.
Copyright © 2020 by Abdo Consulting Group, Inc. International copyrights reserved in all countries.
No part of this book may be reproduced in any form without written permission from the publisher.
Big Buddy Books™ is a trademark and logo of Abdo Publishing.

Printed in the United States of America, North Mankato, Minnesota.
052019
092019

THIS BOOK CONTAINS RECYCLED MATERIALS

Cover Photo: efks/Getty Images; Joe Robbins/Getty Images.
Interior Photos: Ben Liebenberg/AP Images (p. 27); Dick Druckman/AP Images (p. 15); Jeff Roberson/
   AP Images (p. 9); Joe Robbins/Getty Images (p. 29); Kevin C. Cox/Getty Images (p. 13); Ronald
   Martinez/Getty Images (pp. 11, 17, 21); Sean M. Haffey/Getty Images (p. 5); Tom Pennington/
   Getty Images (pp. 19, 23, 25).

Coordinating Series Editor: Elizabeth Andrews
Graphic Design: Jenny Christensen, Cody Laberda

Library of Congress Control Number: 2018967164

Publisher's Cataloging-in-Publication Data

Names: St. Sauver, Dennis, author.
Title: Ezekiel Elliott: superstar running back / by Dennis St. Sauver
Other title: Superstar running back
Description: Minneapolis, Minnesota : Abdo Publishing, 2020 | Series: NFL superstars |
   Includes online resources and index.
Identifiers: ISBN 9781532119811 (lib. bdg.) | ISBN 9781532174575 (ebook)
Subjects: LCSH: Elliott, Ezekiel, 1995- --Juvenile literature. | Football players--United
   States--Biography--Juvenile literature. | Running backs (Football)--Juvenile literature. |
   Dallas Cowboys (Football team)--Juvenile literature.
Classification: DDC 796.3326409 [B]--dc23

CONTENTS

★ ★ ★

★ ★ ★

Superstar Running Back 4

Snapshot 5

Early Years 6

Starting Out 8

Big Dreams 12

Going Pro 14

A Rising Star 18

Off The Field 22

Giving Back 24

Awards 26

Buzz 28

Glossary 30

Online Resources 31

Index 32

SUPERSTAR RUNNING BACK

Ezekiel Elliott is a star running back in the National Football League (NFL). He plays for the Dallas Cowboys in Texas. He began playing **professional** football in 2016. Many believe that Ezekiel is one of the best players in the NFL.

SNAPSHOT

NAME:
Ezekiel Elijah Elliott

BIRTHDAY:
July 22, 1995

BIRTHPLACE:
Alton, Illinois

POSITION:
Running Back

COLLEGE TEAM:
Ohio State Buckeyes

CURRENT TEAM:
Dallas Cowboys

EARLY YEARS

Ezekiel was born in Alton, Illinois. He grew up in a very athletic family.

His father Stacy was a linebacker for the University of Missouri football team. His mother Dawn was a high school state **champion** in three sports. Ezekiel has two sisters, Lailah and Aaliyah.

DID YOU KNOW?

Ezekiel's sister Lailah is a track star. She competed for Ohio State University, just like her brother.

Where was Ezekiel Elliott born?

CANADA

UNITED STATES OF AMERICA

MEXICO

Wisconsin

Lake Michigan

Iowa

Illinois

Indiana

Alton

Missouri

Kentucky

N
W   E
S

STARTING OUT

Ezekiel attended John Burroughs High School near St. Louis, Missouri. He participated in football, basketball, and track. He was a very fast runner, so he excelled in track.

In tenth grade, Ezekiel won the state **title** for the 110-meter hurdles **competition**. He also finished second place in the 300-meter hurdles event.

Ezekiel's high school coach was past NFL quarterback Gus Frerotte.

When Ezekiel was a senior, he won four state **titles** in track and field. He set records in the 100- and 200-meter dash events.

He also set records in the hurdles. For his efforts, Ezekiel won the Gatorade State Track Athlete of the Year Award.

DID YOU KNOW?

Ezekiel's grandfather played basketball at Drake University.

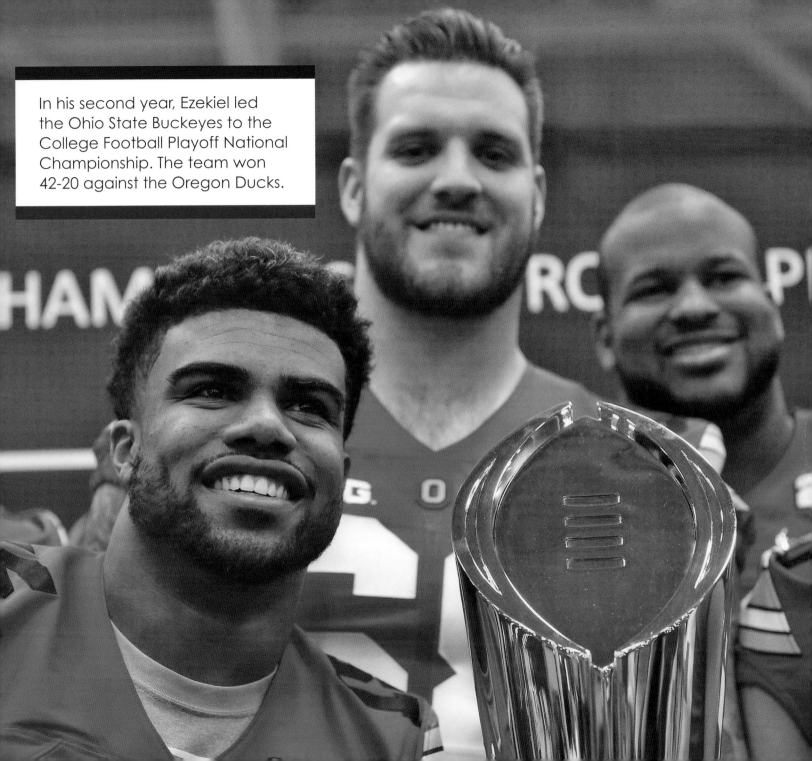

In his second year, Ezekiel led the Ohio State Buckeyes to the College Football Playoff National Championship. The team won 42-20 against the Oregon Ducks.

BIG DREAMS

Ezekiel was an even better football player. He was big, strong, and fast. These skills made him hard to tackle, so he became a star running back. As a senior, he had more than 3,000 all-purpose yards (2,743 m) and scored 50 touchdowns.

After high school, Ezekiel chose to play football at Ohio State University. The college is known for its football program.

By the time he finished college, Ezekiel had gained 3,961 rushing yards (3,622 m).

GOING PRO

During his college years, Ezekiel won many honors. As a sophomore, he earned the Sugar Bowl Offensive **Most Valuable Player (MVP)** Award.

He won the College Football National **Championship** Offensive MVP Award that same year. He was also considered for the 2015 **Heisman Trophy**.

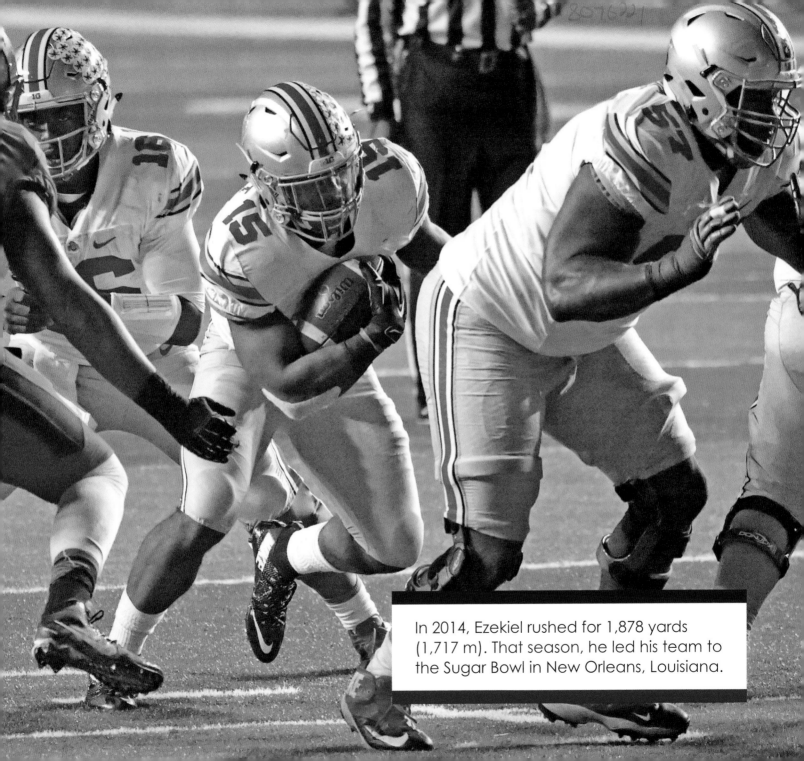

In 2014, Ezekiel rushed for 1,878 yards (1,717 m). That season, he led his team to the Sugar Bowl in New Orleans, Louisiana.

The Dallas Cowboys **drafted** Ezekiel in 2016. He was chosen fourth. That means that the Cowboys thought he would be an excellent player from the start.

Ezekiel **rushed** for more than 1,500 yards (1,372 m) in his **rookie** season. He did so well that he was named to the **Pro Bowl** after his first year.

Ezekiel has great hands. Out of 40 games, he only lost three fumbles.

A RISING STAR

In 2017, Ezekiel continued to impress fans, coaches, and teammates. He scored seven touchdowns and gained nearly 1,000 yards (914 m) **rushing**.

That year, he also caught 26 **passes**. By his second season, he was a valued player for both running and catching passes.

NFL players vote for the Top 100 players each year. In 2017, Ezekiel took seventh place!

Ezekiel's receiving numbers continued to rise. He had more than 1,000 total receiving yards (914 m) by his third season. His bursts of speed allowed him to gain yardage very quickly. He also began to take more of a leadership role within his team.

DID YOU KNOW?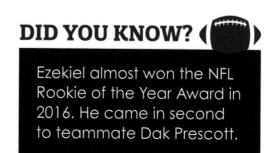

Ezekiel almost won the NFL Rookie of the Year Award in 2016. He came in second to teammate Dak Prescott.

In 2016, Ezekiel helped his team win the NFC East Division title.

OFF THE FIELD

⭐

Ezekiel spends much of his free time working out to keep in shape. He also studies the Cowboys' playbook and film of past plays to prepare for game time.

He loves taking care of his dog Ace. In 2016, Ezekiel wore **cleats** with his dog's face on them. It was for the My Cause, My Cleats campaign. He **supported** the SPCA to bring **awareness** to animal wellness.

Ezekiel likes to watch basketball when he is not playing football.

GIVING BACK

Soon after he joined the NFL, Ezekiel started raising money for the Salvation Army. By the end of 2018, Ezekiel and his fans **donated** $21,000 to the **charity.**

Later, the Cowboys team matched the donation. In total, the Salvation Army received $42,000 because of Ezekiel's efforts.

Ezekiel jumped into a red Salvation Army bucket after scoring a touchdown.

AWARDS

Ezekiel has earned many awards throughout his **career**. In 2014, he was named to the Big Ten Academic All-**Conference** team. That means he earned top grades and performed well on the field.

He also won Big Ten Offensive Player of the Year honors in 2015. Ezekiel later played in his first NFL **Pro Bowl** in January 2017.

Ezekiel was only a rookie when he played in his first Pro Bowl. He was also in the January 2019 Pro Bowl.

BUZZ

The Cowboys team had three straight winning seasons from 2016 to 2018. With Ezekiel's skill and leadership, many believe that the team will continue to win!

DID YOU KNOW?

Ezekiel led the league with 1,434 rushing yards (1,311 m) in 2018.

The Cowboys won the NFC East Division title for the 2018 season.

GLOSSARY

awareness knowledge and understanding that something is happening or exists.

career a period of time spent in a certain job.

championship a game, a match, or a race held to find a first place winner. A champion is the winner of a championship.

charity (cher-UH-tee) a group or a fund that helps people in need.

cleats a strip fastened to the bottom of a shoe to prevent slipping.

competition (kahm-puh-TIH-shuhn) a contest between two or more persons or groups.

conference a group of sports teams that play against each other and that are part of a larger league of teams.

donate to give away something that helps others.

draft a system for professional sports teams to choose new players.

Heisman Trophy (HAIS-muhn TROH-fee) an award given each year to the most outstanding player in college football.

Most Valuable Player (MVP) the player who contributes the most to his or her team's success.

pass to throw the football in the direction of the opponent's goal.

Pro Bowl a game that features the best players in the NFL. It does not count toward regular-season records.

professional (pruh-FEHSH-nuhl) paid to do a sport or activity.

rookie a player who is new to the NFL until he meets certain criteria.

rush to advance a football by running plays.

support to provide help or encouragement to.

title a first-place position in a contest.

ONLINE RESOURCES

Booklinks
NONFICTION NETWORK
FREE! ONLINE NONFICTION RESOURCES

To learn more about Ezekiel Elliott, please visit **abdobooklinks.com** or scan this QR code. These links are routinely monitored and updated to provide the most current information available.

31

★ ★ ★ INDEX ★ ★ ★

awards **8, 10, 14, 19, 20, 26, 28**

basketball **8, 23**

charity **22, 24, 25**

division **21, 29**

draft **16**

Drake University **10**

family **6, 10, 22**

fans **18, 24**

Frerotte, Gus **9**

Illinois **5, 6**

league **21, 28, 29**

Louisiana **15**

Missouri **8**

Ohio State University **5, 6, 11, 12, 13, 14**

playoffs **11**

Prescott, Dak **20**

Pro Bowl **16, 26, 27**

records **10**

Sugar Bowl **14, 15**

teams **4, 5, 11, 15,16, 20, 26, 28**

Texas **4**

track and field **8, 10**

University of Missouri **6**